Creature Comforts (and other poems)

T.A. Margono

BookLeaf Publishing

Presentation by *BookLeaf Publishing*

Web: www.bookleafpub.com

E-mail: info@bookleafpub.com

ISBN: 978-93-5761-086-5

First edition 2022

DEDICATION

Dedicated to Dr. Benjamin Margono, Ingrid Margono, Pingalita Oenkiriwang

ACKNOWLEDGEMENT

First and foremost, I am thankful to God.

I would like to thank my family - my parents, Iwan and Fifi, and brother George - without whose support I would not be where I am today.

I am also grateful to my friends, in particular Grace Ng who drew the cover art for this book, and Kezia Cahyadi, who has been a constant source of encouragement.

And of course, all you readers, whether you picked up this book on Kindle, a bookstore, or left on a park bench. Thank you for reading.

PREFACE

I had my first writing success at fifteen when an essay I wrote on leadership won an all-expenses-paid summer at the University of Melbourne. I had not, at the time, realized what contest my English teacher had submitted my essay to. Unbelievably, I remained similarly ignorant to the significance and nature of the prize throughout the congratulatory announcements and dinner with university representatives, right up until I flipped through the itinerary on the plane to Australia.

I approached the rest of my writing career a little more purposefully but in much the same spirit- enjoying the process until I stumbled on something I could write home about; Signing up for enough electives that a Minor could conceivably be applied for, instagramming my way into an exemplary publishing internship, which led to subsequent internship focused on putting together a commemorative book for my university's 100th year. (In actuality 104th at that point, but the word "Century" fit far nicer in the book's title)

Then a couple more years and a pandemic passed without any writing. Life has a way of letting the so-called important things balloon and the equally-important but more subtle things, like a love for art, gather dust.

Creature Comforts represents both a reminder to appreciate and a celebration of the latter.

Creature Comforts: Open (I)

Comfort is many things in many stages
Buried face deep in stacks of fictional pages
Smiles and hugs and cheerful green shrubs
These are the comforts in all ages

Comfort is many things as a kid
Finding where lost things are hid
A pirate's treasure in the laundry bin
A detective's find on the TV screen
These are the comforts of childhood

Comfort is many things as a teen
Navigating gangly limbs and anxiety
First kisses, both chaste and obscene
An A on a test and a good college next
A pat on the back and no words to lack
The magical moment of catching social subtext
Pouring into lines of paper, angst and nonsense
These are the comforts of adolescence

Comfort is knowing safety the absence of
feeling safe
Battling invisible fears in God's promised
embrace
Food in the fridge and bills all paid
Knowing there will be another day

With windows tightly shut and pills all flushed
These are comforts of the shadows of adulthood

Girls' Night Out

The blacker the streets become
The sharper my senses grow
As a branch brushes my head
I know I stand at five'zero

I see all the shadows and shapes
I hear the creatures of the night
From either side, the howls of mad delight

My knuckles dig into the scratchy seams of the shapeless hood
That hangs loose above the rubber rings
sweatpants dig into my hips
I am covered head to toe
Sober as a soul crossing the Styx

I'm wishing for a drink of my own to pour
Knowing my shadow has doubled and tripled the last hour.

Glass

I walk on a thick carpet to mask
The clackity-clack of my two-inch heels
And I stay behind a curtain to play
So it is my trumpeting instead of my dress that sways
Accurate judgment, hard-earned and unbiased

You and I, we stand at the base of the narrow stairs
We are the same, from our histories to our records
I may be a half-step ahead
And you barrel on, without upset
Saying I cannot fit in the corridors when I am with child
And you rage when I say my tubes are tied

I create a boardgame, a cure to disease, a chapter in history
You tell the world it's worthless
Attach your name and your tweaked story
And now you say, it's worth millions

But, well, actually
There is no difference

In the things I do and things you say
As you say

Jack: In the Box (I)

Lost things, odd jobs, an unsolved riddle
Leave them all at the door, with the right price
But be warned, not to swindle
Or you'll be made to pay back thrice
- Of-all-trades, Jack

Says the sign hanging from the rusty old tack

The store is large, opulent, gilded-gold
sometimes
Or small, crowded, interesting things hidden
Peeking out of corners, seemingly forbidden
Always coated in frost, no matter the season
Sometimes it is both or neither, ever capricious
As its mercurial keeper, occasionally pernicious

The keeper of the store is said to be:
Young, old, spineless, bold,
Raven-haired, straw-headed, pale-faced,
ruddy-cheeked
Dressed in a jester's hat, and red and black
Wrapped in the finest jewelry, only of royalty
There is only one constant;
The name is Jack

Jack: In the Box (II)

Nailed to the walls, you will see
Golden eggs, singing harps, staffs of ice, woven
in tapestry
In the corners, you will find
Giant bones, spring-heeled shoes, malt-eating
rats, plum Christmas pie
The wares come and go,
Stolen from and swindled back and lost and won
For Jack is foolish, but on his brow sits
Lady Luck's kiss
Jack is an everyman

The keeper of the store is said to have;
Candles in a row, neatly spaced on the floor
For you, good buyer, to jump over with a roar

If all stay bright, the fee is free
The quality of your wish guaranteed

If one goes out, the price is halved
Fingers, not a hand
Six goats, not a dozen

If all candles go out, as happens most often

Pray to God for the right price
Jack deals roulette in luck and lives

They say no one finds Jack's store twice
But it always seems to be the same sort enticed
Greedy, afraid, forlorn, occasionally noble
The desperate, the ready to gamble
All so glum, Jack only wants fun

Jack: & Jill (III)

There are sometimes Jills to Jack
Time and ancestry twist and twist, provides titles so various
Jill, Gillian, Juliane, Julianus
Sometimes a different name altogether, but in spirit still
Jack's Jill

A one-time customer, buying freedom from shackles of a kingdom
Clutching a pail of water, wetting all the candlesticks jumped over
"That's trickery," Jack says, disappointed and impressed, "but a deal's a deal."
Jack shatters the King's crown and pays the brideprice
For this Jill, this (one-)life-time Achilles' heel
(As they say, no one finds Jack's store twice)

Jill is sometimes an assistant at Jack's store
But Jill is more often a memento in tapestry, a sweet-and-bitter reminder

Jack and Jill are kind, twisted, healthy, broken
Demented to each other, or perfect together

Jack and Jill live in the house atop the hill
A queen and a jester, a maid and a knave
Jill is a beauty and Jack is a beast
And Jill plunges a knife into Jack's breast
(Either love or death do the trick; it's the
curse-breaker's pick)
Jack rips up wives and women of the night,
seeking Jill
Jill feeds Jack to her brothers and takes Jack's
fortune and castle

Jack sleeps folded into a shoebox
Cut into pieces from a giant's axe
And next to the box, slightly sparking
Always sits his lantern-head-pumpkin
It is something of a turn-off to women
(But Lady Luck favors him still,
and Jill is not always one)

Jill sleeps in any bed
On mattresses upon blankets upon furs upon a
pea
Under the bridge, called witch or banshee
In the deep woods, clothed in red
A prickly constant; Jill can never stay alone
Always a prince, always a hero, always a wolf
To slay, to trick, to conquer, to love
Sometimes only, when things are off-track
A Jack

Good Morning

"I love you, Jesus"
May be the best thing I learned
To start mornings with

Corinthians 13: The L-Word

The most important thing I might have learned
"Love is patient, love is kind"
Love is reliable in its commitment
A matter of both heart and mind

"Love isn't boastful, or self-seeking"
Of human nature, it is a direct contradiction
Easier to dismiss in favor of retaining
Emptiness in so-called preservation

It is said, "Love protects, trusts, hopes, perseveres"
It is to be learned unending - so clumsy, painful, and awkward
Yet in its commitment "Love never fails"
Not only to God and others, it must also go inward

It takes growing up to admit what is lacking
"If I do not have love, I am simply nothing"

Old & New

Out with the old, in with the new
A novel life, reborn in You

Is optimistically promised
And miraculously fulfilled

The old demons no longer have sway
But, I ask, don't new ones come to stay?

For in the storm's midst
All that I see
Is all that goes awry
And a dollop of guilt

But looking a long way back
The starting line far behind
The rusted old shackles
No longer confine

Inner Coach vs Critic

There is the loud coach
The equally loud critic
Balance - That's the trick

Monster Under the Bed

The greatest fear contended with is that of the
unknown
Though the definition shifts as one inches closer
to grown

Shadows under the bed morph from monstrous
and clawed
To blankets, bottles, trash - a harmless hoard

The fear of fitting in and the accompanying
anxiety
Become solid grasps of one's identity

Yet the monster that under the bed never dies
Only shifts and lies
In wait for the next tragedy
Mercurial and petty, a companion ever so steady

Warps futures from predictable and exciting
To daunting and overwhelming
Events once mundane
To personal trauma, not quite so tame

Tearing down the one lie all cling to for stability
To rely on life, in its inherent predictability

Past Principles

Do you count the moments you can't recall?
A word at the tip of your tongue
A name without a face and a face without a
voice
The feeling of climbing a ladder, missing a rung
Missing pieces buried in the cobwebbed
Back of your head

Have you ever realized how much
Is distorted by memory?
Broken puzzle pieces that never fit, as such

Sand pours through clumsy fingers
Single socks with no pairs

Your entire self at hip-height
Who to speak to, what to write
Things that meant the world at eight
Petty grievances and joyous times
Gone with only traces so minor

Have you ever thought of
How no two recall one thing the same
And so once a moment passes
It can never be reclaimed

Have you ever wondered
What it is you don't remember?
Have you ever thought of
How more slips through the cracks
And the cracks widen
Have you ever feared
Losing all the pieces you believed in?

Do you find yourself
Relying on the things you know happened
Snapshots, posts, resume bullets
Immortalize yourself in gigabytes
It makes you start to wonder

Who are you without these moments?
Do you even remember?

Spinning

They say the world stops spinning
when tragedy happens
If anything, it goes faster,
You at the standstill
Realizing you care the most,
feel the most,
come apart the most

(Of course, it is difficult to know
if others say the same, but don't show
Still, you are realizing,
not ruminating)

And the world spins on unimpeded,
hands of time undaunted

You think everyone can see
The girl lost at sea
The only one to shatter
(But all are trapped in their own mirrors)

"Lead you beside still waters
A feast in the presence of your monsters"
You remember these words that were promised
And rage against them

For your waters are not still
Your monsters seek to kill

You struggle to keep up, dipping below waters
Momentum carries sideways and upwards
So you smile and laugh and perform
Though you are more inclined
To cry and scream

You splash and splash, your boat keeps rocking
(Perhaps some waves are of your own making)

It always takes time to recall
When you hold on long enough
That the world spins and you fall
And you rise
In the hills and valleys you ride
The good, the bad, the rough
There is calm, in some form
Hiding in the eye of the storm

4-7-8

Four in
Hold for seven
Out for eight

The knock on the door grows louder
You close your eyes, cover your ears
Reinforce bad behavior

Four in
Hold for seven
Out for eight

The end of the tunnel
Is a moving target
You step into the end
Bask in the light
Then back into shadows
You tumble

Four in
Hold for seven
Out for eight

You pray and put in the work

Pop the comfort bubble
Squint and open the door a crack
And you pick yourself out from the rubble

Four in
Hold for seven
Out for eight

Wind

Wind blows
Down go the dominos

In the north waters
Waste claims its space
Across the surface

The oceans and skies blacken
The ground fills with blood
The earth has no real Kraken
Yet storms and heat and flood
Do just as well in conveying its discontent

Resources thin, lives in ruin
Disaster strikes, bordering on biblical
Then the opportunistic and despicable
begin exacting their price

Creatures bloat and food chains rewrote
Air thickens and sizzles
A pressure cooker planet with hardly any
drizzles

And choice contributors say,
"It's not my portion

To make this go away."

Wind blows
Down go the dominos

The Old Woman and the Cat (I)

There was once an old woman who had an old cat
The latter gorged itself until it was quite fat
The woman, being quite indulgent
Allowed the cat to grow insolent

Unsatisfied with the food and shelter treated
The cat took more than it needed
It took the birds and fish from their cages
Gnawed on their phalanges
Asked why, the cat continued to feed
And said very simply, "Because I can."

Unsatisfied with the things stolen
The cat took the woman's hair for it to wear
her blood when thirst tugged
her herbs to decorate the curb
her water for its keister

It took and took and took
Until the woman said, "Enough! What more can you want?"

The cat bared its teeth in a greedy grin
"I hunger for everything, down to the root
Your fish, your birds
Your hair and your herbs
Your blood and water to pollute."

The woman said, "But you'll leave me with
nothing, you wicked creature"
For the cat tended to destroy all it took, then
stretch and yawn in leisure.
"Then you'll have nothing left either."

The cat shrugged and picked
From its teeth, bones and a wing
"Then I'll predict,
To the old man's house I'll be marching
Next door - far, far away
And again I'll take as I may."

The Cat and the Mouse (II)

Inside the house, there lived also a mouse
Scampering daily to avoid being trampled
As the cat took and the woman scrambled

For the woman, the mouse did try to help
But its full endeavor was less than stellar
Since it was only a whelp

The mouse confronted the cat; "I live here too."
The cat said to the mouse; "Why should I care for you?"

So the woman withered, the walls grew mold
And she told all her remaining household,
"You should leave, no need to be discreet,
For I will soon be deceased."

The cat said, "I will go to the old man's house, far away,
And I will begin again taking as I may."
"I am small, and the roads are wide," the mouse cried
"Perhaps if you carried me on your back -"
But the cat said, "I do not need to pick up your slack."

"You would hardly feel me," the mouse said. "I
am light."
"I will know you do nothing," the cat said
"Only reap my effort, on my back - a blight."

The mouse said, incensed,
"I would not need to, if you did not treat the old
woman so."
The cat answered,
"That is no longer my problem, you well know."

Creature Comforts: Close

Comfort is many things when you're older
A morning with no aches
Waking before alarms ring
Finding joy in simple things
Walking outside on a sunny morning
Letting True Crime podcasts blare all night
Eschewing sleep for a show hitting just right

Learning to laugh at the mirror once or twice
Realizing life isn't lived on thin ice

Quiet moments when the world doesn't spin quite so quick
Learning lessons that for years never seemed to stick
The way loved ones manage to just click

(Perhaps not quite right, values and ideas a bit to the side
But a click all the same, with little to hide)

Sinking into a full bath topped with white bubbles
Unlearning toxic ways to cope with troubles

Leaving the comfort zone you thought kept fears at bay
These are the comforts in knowing one day
You'll be okay

www.ingramcontent.com/pod-product-compliance
Lightning Source LLC
Chambersburg PA
CBHW062204160726
48282CB00027B/987
9789357610865